LIFE IS AN ADVENTURE

I

Ashwini Kumar Aggarwal

जय गुरुदेव

ISBN13: 978-93-92201-64-6 Paperback Edition
ISBN13: 978-93-92201-65-3 Hardbound Edition
ISBN13: 978-93-92201-66-0 Digital Edition

Title: **Life is an Adventure I**
Author: **Ashwini Kumar Aggarwal**

Printed and Published by
Devotees of Sri Sri Ravi Shankar Ashram
34 Sunny Enclave, Devigarh Road,
Patiala 147001, Punjab, India

https://advaita56.weebly.com/
The Art of Living Centre

https://www.artofliving.org/

22nd October 2021 Guru Ram Das Jayanti, 4th Sikh Guru who built Amritsar, 5th to 10th Sikh Gurus are his direct descendants
Formal Opening of Sunview Enclave Office with Akhand Path
Krishna Paksha, Dvitiya Tithi, Kartik Masa, Bharani Nakshatra
Vikram Samvat 2078 Ananda, Saka Era 1943 Plava

1st Edition October 2021

जय गुरुदेव

Dedication

Sri Sri Ravi Shankar

who revealed to us the powerful breathing technique
Sudarshan Kriya

an offering at thy lotus feet

Acknowledgements

To all of nature and mankind that has touched, taught, and enlivened me.

To the five great elements that make up my body physics,

to my *antah karana* that reflects my consciousness and makes me appear alive – *jiva* chemistry, and

to Brahman the supreme reality I am infused with and which is my aim as well.

A remake of our book 'Life is an Adventure of Beauty n Grace' without the pictures.
https://www.amazon.com/dp/8195256023/

Prayer

ॐ भद्रं कर्णेभिः श्रृणुयाम देवाः । भद्रं पश्ये माक्षभिर् यजत्राः । स्थिरैरङ्गैस् तुष्टुवा(गुं)सस्तनूभिः । व्यशेम देवहितं यदायुः ॥ स्वस्ति न इन्द्रो वृद्धश्रवाः । स्वस्ति नः पूषा विश्ववेदाः । स्वस्ति नस्ताक्ष्र्यो अरिष्टनेमिः । स्वस्ति नो बृहस्पतिर्दधातु ॥ ॐ शान्तिः शान्तिः शान्तिः ॥

oṃ bhadraṃ karṇebhiḥ śṛṇuyāma devāḥ | bhadraṃ paśye mākṣabhir yajatrāḥ | sthirairaṅgais tuṣṭuvā(guṃ)sastanūbhiḥ | vyaśema devahitaṃ yadāyuḥ || svasti na indro vṛddhaśravāḥ | svasti naḥ pūṣā viśvavedāḥ | svasti nastārkṣyo ariṣṭanemiḥ | svasti no bṛhaspatirdadhātu || oṃ śāntiḥ śāntiḥ śāntiḥ ||

O Divine Light!

- May our ears listen to the sacred and the auspicious.
- May our eyes see the propitious allowing us to come together to partake of wisdom.
- May our limbs be firm and body attuned to long endurances.
- May our senses function with full alertness and May the sense of contentment be strong.
- May our good thoughts form a discus to shield us and
- May our education give us a shining personality.

Peace in our heart, in our body and in our environs.

Contents

Preface

Expression is a blueprint in the genes. Genes express through the body, the mind, and the tendencies.

Does one know that one is UNIQUE? There just isn't anything or anyone in this creation that is an exact match.

Life is a Precious Burning LAMP. Can it glow to diffuse its light and make the ambience BRIGHT?

All live, some learn, few touch the heights. It's our birthright to express and shine, and have our day in the sun.

Om Svasti

Adventure

Adventure is in our genes. To express it is the soul's call, the heart's need, and the only way to satisfy the intellect.

Take out time for it when you are young. Do not let this life pass by without one.

Applause

Applause kindles the life within, and when it comes from the Master, it grants a success that cannot be erased nor side-lined.

When once you can please him, know that he has taken your responsibility, and your life will never be the same again.

Birth

Birth is an event that cannot be remembered, yet it is the most important event in one's life. Once in a while remember your birth and honor your family, the nurses and other people involved and your birthplace.

Celebrating Birthdays with intuition and awareness is a real gift that you can give yourself.

Beauty

The attraction of a Beauty is in the aura made by a glowing heart. Beauty can be in events, it can be in memories, and it is surely evident in nature. Reflecting a cheerful friendliness and a caring belongingness makes you beautiful.

Intellect and Concepts

Knock on the right Door to break baseless concepts and purify the reasoning. Unless you go seeking, you shall not find, and Life shall just be caught up in petty squabbles and never-ending woes.

Life is much bigger than our horizon, always aim to open the gates to infinity. Sri Sri is one master we can turn to without inhibition. His door opens easily, and his glance bores through the intellect, fashioning it anew.

Smile

A smile is worth a thousand words. Smile from the core of your heart, your eyes shining and cheeks radiating. Smiling helps to achieve the impossible.

Watch any happy child's face, it's full of a winsome smile, that's what makes life charming, that's what makes troubles disappear.

1 NATURE'S BOUNTY

Blossoms

Beauty is in the eyes of the beholder. Flowers still the racing mind; their fresh fragrance can awaken the Divine. Make a habit to plant a sapling and watch it blossom to the fullness of Life. That in turn shall nurture your own Beauty.

Sunrise

Wherever you stay, make it a point to greet the Sunrise. It shall instill the eternal in your soul. Without this, even the soul perishes with the body. Such souls never see the light of wisdom that is not what a human life is for.

The Sun has been worshipped for eons, do not fool yourself that the neon lamps and led bulbs or vitamins and energy drinks are any match for its healing prowess.

Sunset

Gaze long and lovingly at the Sunset. If you do not make such effort, or give elaborate reasons that you don't have the chance due to work commitments, time shall always hang heavy, in moments of peril none shall come to your aid.

Nature has hidden messages that cannot be learnt in the best schools, what nature can teach no man can. Suryavanshi is a technical Sanskrit term in honor of those who allow the Sun to power their lives.

Golden Glow

The spectrum of the setting sun is the light that is utterly soothing. Its color and tone and warmth are very pleasing. Can we have a room with such wavelength in our home? Can we buy such light bulbs and lamp shades to soothe and soften, to nurture compassion, kindness and gentleness?

Moonrise

The light of the moon is known to nourish all plants, and produce vitamins and nutrients in them.

Open your eyes to the moon, and you shall always be talented, men shall envy your skills, and your status shall remain intact in society.

Chandravanshis are those who maintain their cool in the midst of difficulty, take life as a play, and walk lightly on this planet.

Moonset

Make it a habit to watch the moon and let the moonlight enter your eyes. It opens many windows for the soul and enriches one with divine talents.

Previously men used to do many things by moonlight, we seem to have forgotten their wisdom in our nocturnal obsession with smart gadgets.
Never mind, the moon is here tonight too to reconnect and get refreshed. Even romance is particularly effective in moonlight, and so is love-making.

Snow Mountain

Snow mountains are a delight for the senses and they clear all the cobwebs from the brain. Spend some time playing in the snow when young, for these activities are out of reach post middle age.

Snow Pines

Pine trees in winter must be explored as that is the time when our intellect yearns to spend time outdoors and correspondingly the body also renews.

We can opt for visiting the hills and snow laden tracks during the summer holidays or also during the winter breaks. The fresh air fills our lungs and rejuvenates our organs. The strenuous walks build our muscles and keep our joints lubricated. Emotional outbursts and frustrating moods can be bid goodbye in such pristine surroundings, the mind feels empowered to break tiresome habits.

It is an opportunity for love to spring forth.

Snow Flakes

Fresh falling snow has tremendous healing powers, no wonder the ancient hermits often trekked to the Himalayas. Nowadays we have modern transport and proper boarding and lodging facilities, make sure to go on such outings to get renewed, refreshed, and realigned.

Giloye Amrut balli

For many years the humble creeper called giloye or amrut balli graced our home entrance. It used to give bright red buds and its leaves were heart shaped. Long after we heard its immune building and illness prevention properties, as the news channels made it a fashion to advertise giloye juice and giloye vati and giloye churna.

Sky Watching

The sky holds a billion galaxies and infinity beckons the adventurer. Take out your telescope to connect with space, with distance, and with your eternal nature.

Rainbow

Rainbows are natural phenomena that foretell some divine message and are a delight to behold.

River Mountain

Or spend time with river mountains. Pitch a tent for a weekend to experience the deep secrets in the inner recesses of the heart, as revealed by the flowing waters and the steady peaks.

Forest Stream

A narrow forest stream is as exciting as the huge ocean. It evokes an attraction and strikes up a friendship with the adventurer who dares to step out of his narrow confines.

A waterway is a big draw for the evening shoppers or the strollers, who are looking to flock someplace that has flowing water.

Ocean

Oceans cover a great part of planet earth and are teeming with life forms having characteristics that are still a mystery. Even the ocean currents and forces are not fully understood, many tales related by sailors are beyond scientific analysis.

The blue waters are the symbol of the blue sky which is a symbol of Krishna or the unfathomable lord and his mysterious ways.

Trees

A healthy clump of trees builds up the oxygen for a large section of the population, and restores parity with nature. Wherever whenever possible, do plant a tree, and care for it till it takes a firm footing.

Planting trees may seem a thankless chore, but in due time they grow tall and bless all of humanity. Every part of a tree is invaluable, our homes couldn't be made without them

Golden Corn

Corn golden hued is the tangible nourishment for both body and mind. Enjoy such pleasures when the teeth are healthy, or ensure that you never damage your teeth by stupid soft drinks, unseasonal ice, or refined sugars.

Hawkers ply their trade selling sand roasted cobs, or we can steam them and have a corn-on-the-cob. Popcorn is a favorite during movie time on the big screen, take out time to see how it is grown and how soft and inviting the tender bushels are.

2 FORGOTTEN RITUALS

Rangoli

Freedom is being able to do simple tasks every day, being cheerful at heart, sound in mind, and having a functional body. Some people call it happiness, but Liberty to think, speak and act, within your home and at your office is real freedom.

Making rangoli or decorating your house, singing to your heart's content, spending time with friends, walking or doing gardening (minus the phone), these are the flavors of freedom we must all experience.

Rudra Abhisheka

Pouring water over one's head, fresh cool water trickling down the spine. The racing mind freezes, frayed nerves heal, the body springs back to solid action.

Mundan Ceremony

Some ceremonial traditions are an amazing gift of the ancient seers. Mundan or shaving the head at a young age was supposedly to 1) imbibe wisdom, 2) have healthy hair, and 3) keep the ego in check. All three a top priority in today's age.

Sandhya Vandanam

Take out time to honor the dawn, the noon and the dusk. Stop the official tasks and devote time to the surreal rituals, whether meditation, or puja or taking the wife out shopping or playing a game with the children.

Quickly you shall notice the impact, instead of losing something, you shall become the victor of a lot of things. Time pays you back if you respect it, these times have been designed by nature for the surreal and not for earning the bread.

Honor the Dawn, Noon and Dusk with Gayatri Japa or your favorite mantra.

Nadi Pareeksha

Getting to know one's native constitution and what foods one's body digests well and what foods it cannot assimilate is an intelligent investment to make.

Since our moods vary like the seasons, consulting a vaidya off and on and taking pancakarma massages regularly is highly recommended.

Fresh Buns

Cooking and Baking are a delight, and eating fresh buns is heavenly. Make a point to sometimes pitch in in the cooking, and make it a point to eat fresh food often.

Fresh Milk

Milk is another delicacy that has innumerable benefits. Desi cows or pure-bred Indian cows give the most nourishing milk, and it makes sense to visit a goshala and be in the aura of innocent beings.

Ritual

Rituals are everyday processes akin to bathing and wearing fresh clothes that keep the Divine spark brightly lit within. Without ritual, life is meaningless, forlorn, prone to uncertainty and boring.

Rituals have been practiced by humans ever since the beginning of time, and their performance connects us to something beyond dividing lines. Rituals melt our inhibitions, and are essential for the growth of young minds.

Agnihotra Yagna

From the Mundaka Upanishad, the Agnihotra Yagna is easy to do, popular across the globe, and a great healing practice.

Traditional Wear

Dresses worn by village people or hill folk emit a subtle signal that helps in effusing harmonious light wavelengths. Once in a while use fancy dresses and traditional costumes to connect to the colors in creation, and know that we are all One.

Grain Grinding Stone

A stone *atta chakki* used to be a common sight in every home a few years ago. It helped keep the muscles strong, the mind clear, and made nourishing flour that formed the basis of our main meal.

Balloons

Balloons are another expression of joy and festivity. They charm the young and old alike. They make the effort seem effortless.

Celebrate a birthday with purple balloons that almost take forever to blow air into.

Guru's Feet

Feet and the big toe are the organs from where *Narayana* radiates. It is a great fortune and augurs well for the family to wash the Guru's feet.

We may not all get such an opportunity, so the ancients made Guru Puja as an equivalent practice. Whether you perform the puja or participate in one, know that your needs have been addressed, your queries have been resolved, and you have been taken care of fully.

The Path

Some of us seek the supreme path, few of us find it too. The Master illumines it well. Take out time to meet him and his gaze shall get the job done.

Honey Bath

Bathing is not a shower in a jiffy. The Rudra Puja teaches us to have a deeply cleansing bath. Use almond oil to massage the head. Use coconut oil to lubricate the private parts. Use mustard oil to massage all joints, including nabhi, nasika and earlobes. After the bath dry each organ well, even toes, spine and hair.

Colors of Holi

Holi is a festival to break mental shackles. Water and color when applied to the body in a carefree spontaneous manner, gives a message to the soul to free itself from unnecessary protocols and rise above the challenges of everyday pressures.

It is rather awkward to indulge in such rioting when old, since the touch and banter of the opposite sex is involved, so ensure that you do not miss out in your youth.

Fresh Juice

Fresh juice is a great tonic for daily use. It will aid your attitude and your perspective; it will help in keeping the mind pure.

It is a service to the marginal bread winners who wait for someone to ply their trade.

Sugarcane juice with lemon and mint and ginger on a long drive quenches thirst admirably and rejuvenates as well.

Painting

Many children have painting as a hobby, and the renaissance period threw up some of the best painters in the world.

A picture speaks a thousand words, a painting depicts an entire scene and relates a complete story.

Get your colors and a piece of hand-made paper and start sketching. Use water, acrylic or oil paints and soon you will be looking at a masterpiece that will become the pride of your home.

3 SHAD VIKARAS – SIX TOUGH TEACHERS

Envy

An oft quoted *shad vikara* is Envy that causes a malfunction of one's digestive system. It is simply the downward movement of energy at the Manipura Chakra.

Envy is rare amongst siblings when children, and only surfaces as one struggles to find a foothold in society. Treat is as a commonplace trait that can be overcome by surrendering to one's Guru.

Pride

Another *shad vikara* is Pride or undue self-importance. A major component of one's ego, and a necessary trait, it can sometimes become over-whelming.

Simply surrender to the Master, and the pride turns into love and acceptance and powers our goals.

Guilt

Guilt is the trigger of hidden consciousness. It means that we are alive and human. When it persists for too long, then go to the Master and give it to him.

The pain caused by guilt is irreversible, medicines and work cannot be the solution. Guilt gives the soul a harsh beating, only a genuine prayer can address it.

Infatuation

Something that wraps and blurs the intellect is *moha*, a common *shad vikara*. Principally towards our children or loved ones, it is the most difficult to overcome, and takes many lifetimes to weaken. Just accept it and enjoy its tremendous hold.

Greed

A dangerous principle of creation, yet much touted and emphasized in advertisements and marketing banners.

Greed should be directed towards creating and preserving Natural beauty, in sports or music or other creative works, then it retains its rightful place out of harm's way.

Lust

Pranayama or Sudarshan Kriya is an antidote to keeping lustful tendencies in check. Passions are necessary in life, but need to be properly directed when aroused.

Lust surfaces if suppression or denial are applied for too long, then it becomes like a raging storm that leaves wreckage in its wake.

Anger Aggression

An emotion seen in early childhood is Anger or Aggression, which is basically frustration at not having a need fulfilled, seen when a loved one is available for it to be expressed. Anger if allowed to erupt frequently forms neural pathways in the brain that become a dangerous hurdle to life and wellbeing. A little bit of harsh treatment akin to surgery is necessary to curb such an emotion. Ignore him, allow him not an inch of sympathy, and let him realize it doesn't pay to get angry.

Anger is the root of all illness, it is flaunted so much in movies, TV serials and children's games that mankind has become its absolute slave. Households and family members have come to believe it is their birthright to behave angrily, offices and work places and parliamentarians think aggression is the only way. The media is its biggest prey and hostage, newsmen and anchorwomen have sworn to feed it continuously.

Danger

Danger is nature's sign that things are not right internally and a warning to mend one's ways quickly. Sometimes danger is external, but such moments are rare and then help is sure at hand. Weeding out one's anger and aggressive nature is the only way to prevent or overcome danger. Danger is a manifestation of the fundamental laws of nature and if one doesn't wake up in this lifetime, then another results.

Pain

It is Painful to be put behind bars, to which pets are subjected to the most. Cannot be always avoided but unknowingly you are piling up poor karma as a result.

Free the souls or donate them whenever you end up tying them too long or too much pain shall come calling someday. Remember that all pain is self-inflicted.

Intoxicants

If you wish to be intoxicated, allow yourself to be immersed in devotional singing. Any other type of stuff will be a big mistake which only the soul after dropping the body shall realize.

In other words, misdirected intoxication cannot be addressed during one's lifetime.

Bad Company

Friends and Family and Relatives and office Colleagues can show up as bad company in Life. With whomsoever one spends more time, over time he rubs off on us.

Watch it if you are continuously miserable, ill, or complaining. Break the company you are attached to and get over it. Call it quits early or you shall get acquitted of Life later.

4 ELEVATE THE SPIRIT

Clapping

Clapping is a subtle acupressure technique that clears blocked nerves and makes the prana flow equitably in all the *nadis*. Clapping and devotional singing are to be frequently done, never for a moment imagine that good health can be maintained otherwise.

Singing

Sing as if only the divine is present, sing as if you are alone. Singing helps to elevate the soul, singing is the antidote and the balm. Singing is the delight for all.

Laughter

A belly full of Laughter banishes toxins from the gut for a whole year. Genuine laughter alone helps, not sarcasm. Spontaneous humor is a rarity, when it surfaces, know that the Lord has manifest.

Yogasana

We must all do stretches, it keeps the joints flexible and the mind amenable. Yogasana differs from gymming, both have their advantages, but if one is looking to tame the mind then gymming falls flat while Yogasana trumps.
Breath focus, attention direction and body alignment, all go together in Yoga.

Loneliness

A long-haul truck is the epitome of loneliness. Doing the same chore over and over again for months on end, with rarely a soul to communion with.

Something can happen, the unknown might connect, keep
the fingers crossed, and your package gets delivered.

Meditation

While a proper facility allows many to meditate, rare are the
ones who actually experience Samadhi. Flowing waters,
serene beaches and quiet surroundings are conducive to
going inwards.

Don't miss such opportunities, just sit and meditate.
Meditation heals many layers of creation; it brings succor to
departed ancestors and provides safety for coming
generations.

Gratefulness

Nature's bounty in the form of fresh food is the one thing to
be grateful for every day, thrice a day or more. If you cannot
be grateful for the food you eat, you shall be taken for
granted by your own intellect and that shall be the end of
any type of joy.

Joy

Real joy is in sharing. Indescribable all-round happiness
results from participating in Yagya, Homa, Havan. Its effects
are subtle as well as profound, and transcend space and
time and government functioning.

For children, the parents and society engineer many events
and parties for the fountain of joy to spring forth, continue
these habits in adult life and old age too. Take out time to
make joy manifest in your parents and grandparents. Lots of

intuition and planning is needed to make an event joyful, it is one of earth's principal gifts to mankind.

Dancing

Dancing is the call of the soul. When the Master dances, the world celebrates, all experience the divine grace. Invisible orbs too make their appearance, devi devata rishi muni, all join in to taste the bliss.

Flight

Space Flight is also a lonely ordeal, but there is more probability to connect to the unknown, the unfathomable, and hopefully become freed in the bargain.

Snow Trek

Trekking in the snow can be refreshing for the senses and healing for the brain. The coolness reaches all corners of the mind, soothes frayed nerves, and helps judicious decision-making.

Rowing

Boating, rowing, or spending time in the waters can uplift the soul and help the intellect overcome the mundane trappings of land.

It makes sense for town planners to make such facilities for our children, especially in cities far from shore. It spurs invention and creativity; it reduces tension and stupidity.

Bhastrika Breathing

And breath is the KEY. The single MOST IMPORTANT learning in Life is learning how to breathe properly. Any other technique like music, sports, trekking, gymming or hard labor is simply designed to tune the breath.

Bhastrika is an astonishing technique to repair all tissues and recharge all cells of the body by doing some forceful breathing to a mathematical count.

Once Bhastrika is perfected, Sudarshan Kriya is the ultimate 10-minute rhythmic breathing system we can all adopt to achieve our goals and lead a happier life.

Rejoicing

Events and Occasions need to be held regularly to engender laughing, singing dancing and clapping. Involve all members of the family and workforce, invite neighbors, friends and relatives, let everyone partake of the bliss.

Dance

Then life becomes a dance. The intellect gets purified. You walk lightly as a cloud. You live each day lit bright.

The seasons celebrate, nature rejoices, and relationships blossom.

Silence

A deep silence for 10 days and no eye contact is the norm during a vipassana course at a Dhammagiri center. If one can survive the initial 3 days of detox, the mind starts to gather strength.

This strength becomes the core strength that forms a long-term shield for the intellect and makes the mind tough to weather storms and trying times. Even the body benefits as illnesses are flushed out and organs get repaired.

River Rafting

If we visit Rishikesh, a fun adventure sport is available. It ain't for the weak hearted, yet it must be resorted to, to break inhibitions and overcome restlessness and mental blocks.

Most of us live a sheltered pampered life, so much so that we never learn skills to evolve and grow out of our comfort zones. When young, go for such an adventure, it shall repay you back manifold as time goes by, hidden fears in the mind shall get erased clean.

Jump High

Show off your youthfulness and your enthusiasm. Take every opportunity to flex your body and express the divinity. Outings help when friends are around, instead of showing off your wealth and possessions, show off what your body can do, and that will stand you in good stead.

5 TRANSFORMING OPEN SPACES

Construction

Making a proper venue for common welfare demands divine vision, astute foresight and inner strength. It is rare to meet men who have been endowed with such a clarity regarding Life.

Praise their work and honor their presence, something magical will surely result in your life as well.

Pools and Fountains

Small pools and fountains help heal and rejuvenate the consciousness. Let each builder make these a part of his colony and keep them clean and well-maintained.

Water bodies

Our body is more than 60% water content. If we have water bodies around us, that resonates within and washes the soul of misery, and intellect of miserable thinking.

Temple Building

A precise science is involved in the making of a Temple. From the spire to the altar, the seating to the stairs, each aspect needs to be thoroughly planned and carefully engineered. Only then the aura of the temple can be inviting to the saints.

If saints do not come to a temple, it cannot serve its purpose, only the feet of the saints make the precincts of the temple divine for the devotees, safe for the children and soothing for the weary.

6 MANKIND'S GIFT

Gadgets

Gadgets have taken control of mankind, and it takes strength and guts to switch them off. Know that prudence in their usage shall empower you to take critical decisions and face menacing challenges.

One's innate wisdom if safeguarded from over indulgence in gaming and social media can do what no gadget can.

Cycle

A new bicycle is every child's dream come true. Soon the dream morphs to become a motorcycle, then a merc, and finally a jet.

Whatever is your dream, if you work for it, you shall manifest it.

Our dads did it before us, and so can we.

Radio

Listening to music alone might be fun, but listening in a group is heavenly.

A radio is the best companion for solitary travelers, drivers and the like, since you can tune to different stations and get fresh content.

Ride

Such a joy to ride on one's bicycle…or any vehicle for that matter. Riding or driving frees the intellect, makes one go ahead of time sorta, and a long drive on a good path is really satisfying.

The intellect discards old plans and makes new ones, the body gets a good appetite, and evolution happens.

New Buy

Such pleasure floods our being when we go shopping and bring home a new buy. When it is bought out of one's first pay, the joy is boundless.

Remember to give back to your parents when you start earning, they have been the cause of multitude pleasures for you in your youth.

Boats

Colorful flags and freshly painted boats make it inviting to have a ride and you shall enjoy the outing thoroughly. It is a fervent prayer that town planners and builders incorporate this facility as it instills certain traits in the young children that are otherwise lacking in the populace living far from the coastline.

Here are a couple of things that a boating trip can awaken in the raw intellect – the swaying rhythm of the ride gives a natural shake to the nerves, loosens some stiff muscles, and frees some ancient memories. The scent of water sprays in the air dislodges respiratory blocks, and can heal the lungs just as a trip to the hills does.

7 REAL ASSETS

Family

Folks with whom we spend the maximum time are family. We rub off on them, they modulate our brain waves, temper our speech, and together much gets achieved.

Parents

Parents are made of sugar and spice and all that's nice. They were the best of the best for us when we were children and the apple of their eyes we were.

Perhaps we can invest in their joys and make occasions to enhance their pleasures.

Father

Father enjoys continuous hard work and is always available to lend a hand.

Mother

A mother's heart is happy in the presence of her children.

It makes sense to visit your mother every now and then, chat and remember old times, play some games and eat together.

Couples

Couples on holiday bring back memories of joint families and smooth team work. Every household chore or office task seems light when done in pairs.

Friends

Friends do spontaneous acts, their presence makes any event joyous, the occasion amazing, and the soul enriched.

Friends2

Friends may not do anything and just be.

Soul Mates

Coming together is a rare occurrence and fragile to boot, feel blessed when your wavelengths match. Know when it is un-hard to jam, and easy to chat on nothing.

Soulmate

Once in a while the magic happens. Minds meet and matter is discarded.

Siblings

While growing up siblings accelerate the creation of neurons and neural pathways, since you can easily mix with them irrespective of age gap or gender, stick to your own point in any debate, and participate in many activities, sports, and outings.

Village Family

Even taking the weekend off to visit a village and spending time with the village folk can bring out our innate finer feelings.

Their hospitality is boundless, their possessions few yet their hearts magnificent.

Family of 4

Families account for all the good times and fun. That may be celebrating birthdays and school functions, or simply eating together on Sundays. Whatever they do, it reverberates across time, it leaves imprints in space, and becomes history.

Neighbors

Growing up with blessed Neighbors is exciting, titillating and utterly satisfying.

The Saint

Arrived 15 Aug 1917 Hamirpur Himachal. Departed 3 Sept 2010 Ludhiana. Ratan Muni Maharaj used to visit our home and take a proffered glass of milk from mother or biji. We used to visit the Jain Sthanak in chaura bazaar regularly and Maharaj ji used to recite the Navkar mantra "Om namo arihantanam" specially for everyone's benefit.

His calm affable manner cheered the devotees, his aura gave immense comfort. I remember visiting him for the last time in 2009, he remembered me and chatted lovingly.

O What a saint, accessible, affordable, personally available and thoroughly caring!

Grandfather

Grandfather was called Big Papa by one and all. But he wouldn't miss playing cricket or a card game, and spent hours on his harmonium. Born Ludhiana 1912 Left Scarborough Canada 1989. Served in Kenya, Ludhiana and Rajkot.

He had spent time in the African outback amidst lions, and enjoyed aloofness.

Biji

Grandmothers have more sense than we care to acknowledge, and their experience is priceless. Their presence makes everything function normally, their emotions make the house lively and welcoming.

Bibi

Bibi was a cheerful character whose laughter rang loud and true. She outlived Bauji by a score of years and had to fend for herself many a time. But there was an inner strength that kept here going till the end, a strength that is perhaps lacking in our children who missed out on her touch.

Maa

Maa appeared suddenly out of nowhere and proved that lifetimes exist that are from another era or a forgotten place.

8 PRIMAL INSTINCTS

Eagle

An eagle radiates raw power, and instills faith that we can also soar to the higher planes.

We can also have its penetrating clear eyesight, strong foothold, and agile arms.

Langurs

Monkeys of the Langur species have many traits that mimic the human. Social, familial and group activities, and pack Leadership and obey the rules or take punishment if you falter.

It is good to learn from these faunae, it makes sense to spend time with birds and animals and partake of their company.

Snake Charmer

Cobra is a symbol of Alertness and quick Action. If one can harness such values and integrate them in our personality, we can be sure of a successful life, a rewarding reality, and a fulfilling existence.

Just as a cobra sways to the melodious notes of a flute, so also our intellect can be calmed by meditation.

Terrier

Terriers can evoke this bond and make us experience compassion. From nowhere they appear, they do what no pet can.

Pony

Watch a pony cropping grass. Or take him for a ride.

Establish communion with nature that is divinity at its best.

Grazing

We have been grazing for lifetimes after lifetimes. The divine has been fortunate to bless us with a human sheath. It is time to seek the supreme. Make the ultimate your topmost aim.

Let not this life pass by in eating and entertaining and other frivolous pursuits.

Butterfly

Watching a colorful butterfly flitting from flower to flower. Who makes its wings pretty? Who gives it such agility? Who allows it to taste nectar?

Does he also know about Me? Does He care?

9 WHO AM I

Even animals ponder and stop to exercise their grey cells,
we as humans must certainly pause and reflect.

Not just in difficulty or when puzzled, but

again and again
seek answers to the profound questions

WHO AM I, WHAT IS ALL THIS, WHY AM I HERE?

10 Freedom

What is Freedom? Have you ever wondered?

- Is it just having your pockets full and being able to shop till you drop? Is it just marrying the girl of your choice or winning Wimbledon? Is it that simple?
- Is it based on monetary or momentous events to brag about?

Freedom is knowing that every wish gets granted, so we must be very careful in desiring. Freedom is in living within limits and following protocols and standards.

Freedom is knowing how much to eat and what to eat, keeping in mind body disposition and digestion.

Freedom is knowing that one is eternal, so is there any need to be rushed, be agitated, or bend the rules.

Freedom is knowing that the senses are turned outward, hence they need to be kept in balance to prevent drowning.

Freedom is assimilating Einstein's theory of relativity, understanding that time and space are fickle concepts and not absolute, so we can reach the ends of time and cover all of space someday. But that can happen only with self-Discipline and mature Responsibility.

Freedom is the disconnection from pain.
It is knowing that

- Truth overcomes lusT

- Ahimsa subdues greeD

- envY is vanquished by Gratefulness

- infatuation mohA dissolves in *samadhan* Contentment

- angeR cannot face Kindness

- pridE is flattened by Humility

It is realizing that Infinity ∞ is within zero, and zero O is the source of infinity.

ॐ

पूर्णमदः पूर्णमिदं पूर्णात् पूर्णमुदच्यते ।

पूर्णस्य पूर्णमादाय पूर्णमेवावशिष्यते ॥

ॐ शान्तिः शान्तिः शान्तिः ॥

11 Who Is GOD

The standard definition is all knowing, most powerful, and present everywhere. *An energy being (light body) that forms out of Brahman time and again.*

Let us see what is the meaning of **all knowing**. It means that GOD can analyze and understand any situation, see through any pretense, and knows all the principles and science thoroughly. It does **not** mean that he is forever analyzing everything.

Most powerful. God is stronger and more skillful and intelligent than anyone else. But it does **not** mean that he is trying to subdue or overcome anyone.

Present everywhere. He can manifest anywhere and concurrently at will.

However, he surely does **not** idle his time at all places all the time. Like air is present everywhere, but a fan whirrs for a while and not in all places all the time.

So much for the standard definition. If you look closely, this definition nowhere mentions anything about right/wrong or good/evil. It means these are local concepts, based on a particular point-of-view, which may not remain constant. So, if we try to limit and capture GOD within one's own definition of what is happening and what should happen, what is kindness and what is cruelty, it will certainly be naïve and untrue.

What must be understood here is that GOD or Brahman espouses both zero and infinity, and the entire spectrum within and without. So various flavors, colors, emotions, and principles manifest for a while, and then go out of fashion. It is a sinusoidal reality, with crest and trough and the intermediate peaks and valleys.

This is commonly known as OPPOSITE VALUES ARE COMPLEMENTARY IN CREATION.

Nothing is fixed; change is a constant reality as observed in galaxies.

All the same, Scriptures lay down guidelines for **proper** living. Herein *proper* to mean a life which has **minimum** of turmoil and sorrow. If someone follows the scriptural injunctions correctly (open to debate but generally you must follow your Guru or King), that soul is largely safe from challenges that he cannot handle, or adequate help arrives in time for him.

However, know that creation will always have forces that are much more powerful than you, hence the need to be humble and grateful and accepting. Never ever think you are GOD, or that you can do anything.

At the same time know that there is someone who **loves** you, whether someone calls you a Saint, or the world treats you like a sinner, there is definitely someone who bats for your, cheers you and treats you as his very **own**.

Lastly keep in mind that anything born has an exit, we as humans depart after 400 years irrespective of the way we lived. GOD is simply the energy that manifests within us to make us light, cheerful, well, able, and is available to all of us.

12 EDUCATION

Gurukul

A place where age, background, economic status or standing in society is shelved and all go through the same drill is called a Gurukul. Somethings the younger ones are good at, other tasks the elderly are proficient in. It really doesn't matter. Just being together is the key, melding and working as a group. Learning things that may never be needed, but learning to do things jointly is the principle. Nature automatically creates hilarious, thorny, or impossible situations and all benefit immensely.

Thinking

Thinking is an art you need to get thoroughly trained in. It needs proper company and a peaceful environment, and it needs patience and endurance. *Generally, our mind is used to emitting strings of words that are hinged in the past based on impure memory, or trying to day dream of the future based on impractical reality.*

We need to align our needs and desires with our resources, skills and present circumstances.

How may we do that? Just producing random or fanciful or fearful thoughts is a serious strain on the nervous system, that in turn leads to various imbalances and poor health. Do you think our educational system or our temple system or our work culture or our shopping marketplace is teaching us the correct methods?

There are very few organizations that address this paradigm. You will need to find out and learn the correct techniques. The Art of Living Foundation is doing an admirable job in this area through many programs for all segments of society. Perhaps it is a wise move to culture your thinking, and it is never too late to educate yourself on this aspect. https://www.artofliving.org/in-en

Brahmins

Being a Brahmin means spending time learning the scriptures, doing lots of physical chores, playing games and music, and serving the Master.

Pathshala

A *pathshala* is aptly named, a room where recitation is done, which leads to various paths, a place that has endless possibilities. What you do there doesn't matter, neither what you don't do. It just matters that you go through it, and unknowingly pick up life skills.

Foundation Stone

When a new institution is made and a foundation stone is laid, no one knows what the outcome will be. Many years pass before the laurels come, before the faculty and alumni begin to get praised, and the institute becomes revered and sought for.

Thought

Thought for the day is a common sight at the entrance of most temples in India.
For those who prefer home delivery, the mobile apps update it daily as a new thought gets pasted. For those who prefer a years' guide, books are available. The important point to note is that what strikes a chord must be copied and written down, underlined and highlighted, reflected upon and assimilated.

Teachers

And my teachers were certainly divine, there is no doubt of that.

Classmates

Many a time I have felt that my classmates throughout school, college and university were hand-picked by the lord to keep me safe and out of harm's way. I could be doing my own thing in my own shell that had little bearing on practical reality and that was far removed from what was happening around me (or in society as a whole).

High School

Ever Onward they say is the motto of Life. Is schooling enough to lead there? There has to be a strong vision, a burning passion, a fierce ambition. And how can it be kindled?

Company of the wise. Company of the brave. Company of someone who has made it there.

Protected

Protection cannot be had by steel doors or surveillance cameras or big locks alone. A Master's care is the ultimate protection that is invisible yet always functioning.

13 One needs LOVE ATTENTION APPRECIATION

Hak हक

Hak is a beautiful word that signifies a loving ownership.

Who to own is immaterial. In creation there are sights and sounds, nature and humans, machines and toys, emotions and principles. Do not let this life pass by without hak, saying no one loved me, no one wanted me, nothing appealed to me, or that I was useless.

Life is a fluid mixture and a veritable melting pot where many opportunities present themselves to take ownership, exercise responsibility, or be useful. Some people think that *hak* can be applied only to pets or toys, hobbies or food, furniture or gadgets. So, what, go ahead and do it. At least exercise your right and know that you are in-charge.

What if seasons change and the object changes? Let it be. Don't miss it. Just DO IT.

Teenagers

Teens love to pose and that is the age when one may do anything (by law).

Letter

23/6/84

Dear Ashwini,

It's really been a very long time since we heard from you. It's a bit disappointing that we have had no news from your side since long.

First of all I would like to wish you on your 19ᵗʰ (? 1965) birthday. May you be able to fulfill all your hopes and ambitions as you enter this new year of your life. And may God bless you and always remain by your side. These well wishes come to you from all of us including Shilajeet, Kinkini and their family (since there is no guarantee that their letter reaches you — our 'highly efficient' postal service and also due to the disturbeed conditions in Punjab.

All of us had been to Pune for 4 days and we enjoyed the change in surroundings. I have started playing billiards since 12/6/84 and yesterday made my first over 10-point break. I scored 13 points in one chance. Shilajeet had been here on 15/6. His college started on 1/6. Monty's college starts on the coming Monday while Kinkini will join in a few days' time. My institute reopens on 25/7.

Shilajeet was supposed to write a letter to you in the recent past. Hope it reached you. We would be expecting an ...

The places. His new address is

A-004, Neelkanth ~~Apartments~~ Society
Shivaji Road
Ambernath
421503

With warm regards to your parents
and love for your sisters and expecting a long and detailed
letter from you.

Yours affectionately,

Nitin

<u>P.S.</u>

Our school's S.S.C. topper scored 89.86%. Mr. Fernandes
had taken up the post of a Principal in a Goan school last
year. The new Principal has introduced radical changes.

Nitin

Mr. ASHWINI KUMAR
House no. B-IV, 734
MALI GANJ CHOWK
LUDHIANA
PUNJAB 141008

From
A-3/7, CRC
SHAHAD
421103

Soul

None hath seen the soul, though many have experienced its presence. Its glowing light is fragile and easily dimmed. Only the Master can keep it lit, only the Guru can make it blossom. In this life, make that a wish.

Again and again have the company of the Master, again and again partake of his Satsang.

Birthday

Unplanned birthdays afford the greatest surprise and hence deliver the maximum delight. Birthdays and anniversaries are the days to look back and be grateful for our achievements. And see if we can drop some habits and inculcate new ones.

On such occasions the mind gets transported back, the memories flood the being, and the time is ripe for renewed courage, vision and principles to be harnessed.

Prize

All of us have been awarded in school or college for one thing or another. The prize moment is rare and does something wonderful to the soul.

Even for a regular champion, such a moment is to be treasured and kept alive, albeit discreetly without flaunt.

Team Project

Teams and Projects with common goals are what make businesses flourish. Involve yourself in large team projects that have a spectacular vision for mankind. Be clear of the direction in which the top management is headed, only then pitch in.

If you make money your primary motive, or become collateral for dubious gains, justice shall catch up with you before you die, and it shall be painful in the extreme, and no amends can be made then.

Buckle up and U-turn to change companies whenever the management policies become murky, the world has more opportunities than pitfalls.

Diwali

Diwali is the festival of lights and victory of good over evil. It is the homecoming of a just king and the joyous celebration of *Ram Rajya* or good times.

Life that stopped; becomes meaningful because we clean our homes, dust and wash from top to toe and discard the torn and broken. We buy new gifts and usable items, distribute sweets and exchange pleasantries.

Ganesh Laxmi Puja signifies clearing of all obstacles and showering of all wealth.

Belly Full

No matter what we do, where we live, or what our goals are, we all crave a belly full. Once it's had, the soul's renewed, the heart finds love.

Romance

Romance and its excitement are short lived but its effects last a lifetime.

Food is first love and then a regular old-fashioned romance.

Marriage

The occasion of tying the knot makes the entire community rejoice. Everyone gets to lend a hand in the innumerable tasks that make the event a resounding success showering blessings on the groom and the bride and their parents.

Cricket Eleven

A cricket team has eleven players and five more on the bench for substitute fielding and rotation during various matches. Life has eleven members in the form of the 5 senses and the 5 organs of action and the 11th is the mind as Captain.

When our habits cause some breakage, we also add substitutes in the form of spectacles, pacemaker, knee caps, walking stick and dentures. It is good to maintain hygiene and discipline so that substitutes can be postponed till old age. Needs lots of courage and guts though to follow the fitness path and not deviate from it.

1 + 1 = 11 as India leads the way in World Cricket
Championships

Party

Party times are all about dressing up and showing off.
Sometimes a party brightens up the dull moment, but
usually it is just a route to self-damage and self-immolation.
The stuff served during get-togethers is designed by the
devil himself, who makes it a point to rule at such moments,
be it marriages, celebrations, festivities or promotions.

Attitude

You are free to show your attitude amongst friends. Pride
wells up and boosts your morale. Attitude is also good to
cultivate in day-to-day life.

And what kind of attitude?

The one that keeps you humble and down to earth.
The one that keeps you kind and helpful.

14 RISE HIGH IN YOUR PROFESSION

Bhikshus

A simple ceremony practiced variously in many cultures is the opening of the gates of the intellect to higher knowledge. Our seers devised it to make man amenable for a bigger role in society, to care for our fellowmen, and to move simply in society.

Mataji

She lives a solitary life in a sparsely inhabited deep jungle where she is both the law and the strongman rolled in one. Such souls manifest to tune the path, prune the pathways and highlight some talents. Sanskrit is her guiding passion, and that is a refreshing break when compared to so many other disciplines. May her disciples grow and enrich the planet, may her Guru's vision manifest in the populace.

Doctors

Long ago the Indian doctors were held in high esteem. Becoming a doctor was akin to reaching the top of the Pyramid. Now again the profession has regained some respect. The times have swung in their favor, and hopefully doctors can ingrain the ethical principles by letting go of their pharmaceutical bosses and their professional hospitals.

Doctors and the Medical fraternity work tirelessly but seldom get accolades, now is the time to celebrate their gift to humanity and give them due status in society by their own employers and professional institutions.

Relatives

Relatives just happen, there is no choosing. Some principle of physics is in operation here, or maybe it is chemistry.

Ashramites

Buddies, roommates, colleagues or ashramites are handpicked by the Lord to facilitate progress on the path. Even so, discard the chaff from the grain and choose your company with care so that evolution happens and not dissolution.

Wise men

Wisdom comes in many flavors and in all age groups. Every town and village has them, the country keeps going smoothly due to their presence.

Wise woman

Wise women are around us too. Persevere and you shall be granted their beatitude.

Brothers

Brothers can team up to move mountains and turn the impossible into a reality. Our puranas and epics are the source of many fabulous tales depicting brotherhood. Ram and Lakshman, Arjun and Bhim, Luv and Kush.

Administrator

An administrator is someone who can wield the sword and also be peaceful and compassionate at heart.

Peace Forces

Commandos who guard the frontiers and ensure peace between nations are made up of solid frames, brave hearts, and a willingness in shouldering responsibility.

It is such a blessing to be in their company.

Sadhus

In Sanskrit, the word *Sadhu* refers to gentle hearted, compassionate.

Is it that a dress is needed to display kindness?
Or is it that a protocol reminds me not to err?

I don't know.

15 TOUCH THE ANCIENT

Old Fortress

The men who walked before us had legendary construction
skills and splendid vision of form and structure. Make an
effort to imbibe their greatness by visiting historical places,
admiring their handiwork, and soaking in times gone by.

Old Monastery

The 108 pyramid huts and my Master lived in No 13 long ago
in Rishikesh on the banks of the Ganges. Each hut is double-
storied, with a top Meditation room and a bottom sleeping
quarter, with a tiny attached washroom.

Someday when you build your own home, ensure that it has
a place for Meditation, furnished and equipped for deep
thought and purposeful study.

Ancient Carving

Make sure to have a touch of the ancient in your home. Be it
a wood carving, a painting, a sculpture or a fossil. Time is
eternal and so are you.

Connect to respect, imbibe and evolve.

Architecture Grandeur

Time stands still when we stand in front of an architectural
masterpiece. So much effort, so much detail, so much
teamwork and such a wonder to behold.

Give a thought to traditional artists and their skills, make an
effort to keep such detailed precise craftsmanship alive.

16 CLAY POT

I am a clay pot. Fashioned by whom? I do not know? Why?
No idea.

Depending on who gets me, I get filled with water or grain,
flowers or fruits. Sometimes the one who owns me is cruel
and uses me as a dustbin. At other times I am loved and held
on his head.

Light Orbs

A langar at the gurudwara on a poornima is a treat for the whole family. Along with strangers, you rub shoulders with aliens, and feel all are family.

Light Bubbles

Light bodies are usually captured in the dark when stars and planets make their appearance. They have a story to tell, perhaps in time we shall have our own light bubbles for travel.

Light Bodies

Once in a while the camera captures light bodies. Halos with shapes and signatures of another time, another plane, and the surreal. Perhaps they give a message, maybe they are thankful, anyways it signifies something divine.

Lighted Bodies

Sometimes the light bodies leave distinct signatures and patterns. They are souls from another time, or an alien planet, and for sure we shall make contact with them in the near future, say by 2040 AD.

Honey Comb

A single honey comb is the work of hundreds of bees. Similarly, life is a bouquet where each event, each person, and each season fills you with nectar bitter sweet.

Footprints

Life is fragile and it is evident on the sands of time where our footprints last not even an hour. This knowledge when well-assimilated is the Vedanta in Life.

Vision

A sound Vision takes years of discipline to manifest. Do not think that you can make it happen overnight. Have the sense to perfect your vision, have the courage to live up to your ideal. Have the patience to persevere against all odds, the Lord's just waiting to hold you in his arms.

Darshan

This is also known as *darshan* of divine. When the senses get balanced, the hands start working in tandem, and success gets granted.

Birds Three

Three is the principle that keeps balance and this creation going. Sattva Rajas Tamas, Dawn Noon Dusk, three legs of a stool, the past the present the future, call it by any name, find out your own real-life example. The Act of eating, the Food being eaten, and the One eating.

Before

Before and after is a story that unfolds slowly for the builder and his team.

After

It delights the heart and brings souls together as time passes.

Ras Leela

Dancing with the Lord is everyone's dream and a wall-fresco makes it come true.

Radha

Radha is the emotion that evokes the Lord. Radha is the call of the soul and its nourishment too. Radha is symbolized as a maiden who gives the lord bliss and who does his every bidding without tarrying or grumbling.

Tourists

Tourism is another activity that helps clear the intellect of many wrong notions and moves one a bit out of our comfort zones. Again, it works much better when the intellect is raw, since a mature intellect has already carved neural pathways that prevent useful learning.

What makes sense as a child is not of much use to an adult, as the adult mind is trying to see the profit and loss and what will I get out of it and where I should spend and where I should not. Tourism bereft of such thinking alone can be of any value, since it is an activity meant to culture the intellect and broaden one's vision.

Lawn

A manicured lawn is a sight for sore eyes and a terrific acupressure for bare feet.

Lamp

Lamp light brightens the room and is also amazing for the intellect. Our *antah karana* or reflected consciousness is also a frequency of light that benefits immensely from the glow of a lamp or a candle flame.

There are different spectrums of light, cool daylight or warm incandescent bulb, etc. The light that is closer to the spectrum of sunlight has a positive impact on the intellect, as we are biological beings with inbuilt resonance for firelight or sunlight.

दिया तले अन्धेरा is a common Hindi phrase to signify a lamp's glow highlights dark corners in our intellect, and thus can help to overcome them

Xmas

Christmas candles are lit to illumine the intellect and satisfy the divine within.

Perspective

A camel looks so big in front of the Great Pyramid of Giza, Egypt. Matter of perspective. When you look at life from a divine angle, the problems look small and success looms bright. How to improve one's perspective is a challenge. It doesn't happen overnight.

Stick to the premise that life is Perfect, in God's hands, and the best is actually Happening, and that may help to view the situation from another angle. It takes a lifetime to inculcate such practices and assimilate these teachings, but know that life is 400 years long over 7 births in the human plane, and this might be your very first birth.

Rickshaw

Know that you could be paddling a rickshaw, what are you cribbing for? And that too in the scorching suns of a harsh desert. You are just a tourist spending a few hours here, view all of life from this viewpoint.

Of course, it will need some determination and some discipline, it will need a Master and Authentic effort.

Trunk

Tree trunks and elephant trunks have the solidity that one must ingrain in one's spine. The spine supports the trunk of the body, and a solid spine is the basis of a fit mind as well. Here Yogasana shall help, nothing like cobra, cat-stretch, dandasana, boat pose or shoulder-stand to make the spine sturdy like a tree trunk.

Contrast

We all seek contrast, when it is hot the AC is needed, and when it is cold, the geyser. Life has its natural contrast in the form of young and old, light and dark, and accepting and balancing the two is divinity.

Sand

Sand particles are tiny, and contain silica, used in most electronics and gadgets that we can't afford to live without for even an hour.

Open your mind to the possibilities on this planet, and your grumbling shall turn to wonder, your sorrows shall become avenues for success. When one sets the mind on big targets and challenging roles, pettiness vanishes and prudence emerges.

Again and again become a student and look at everything with fresh eyes and a friendly smile. The Lord is not hiding in places of worship, he is all around in each and everything.

Emptiness

Vacuum is the stark reminder of lifelessness. Benches and desks wait for life to occupy them, similarly our body waits till we seek out our Purpose.

Body is the tool, put it to great use, lest it rust away the soul.

Fullness

Spending time with classmates can be a means of approaching life from various angles, where some boys will pull us down, while other girls will pull us up. Both are essential for development and both help us function in real life.

Students wake up in their 12th standard, or do they?

17 ENLIGHTENMENT

Enlightened

Someone asked me, what do the enlightened look like and what do they do? This is my favorite answer, Bharat Bhaiya cooking for us and relating humorous anecdotes. To experience it, one can join the Advanced Meditation Course of the Art of Living.

Another picture is that of Kanwal Didi relating stories from the puranas. Enlightenment happens when we listen to such a discourse from the lips of a Saint and their calm effulgent state of mind filters deep down into the core of one's being.

Vedanta

Is scriptural learning enough? Self-study is of paramount importance. What is heard *Shravanam*, must be reflected upon bit-by-bit Mananam, and

slowly digested by long hours of earnest effort, sincere commitment and Hard karma yoga Niddhidhyasanam.

Entrepreneurs

They look like any other folk in the neighborhood, but inside them is that blazing flame fueled by requisite talent and sound work discipline. It enables them do pioneering stuff and quickly reach the top of the Pyramid. It is starkly evident in their Eyes.

Their company is definitely warranted for anyone aiming to break the mundane shackles and attain to the heights of magnificent achievement.

Monks

Company of monks is a desirable facet of life and must be enjoined at some stage in life.

Tibetan monks at Bodh Gaya, the place of Buddha's enlightenment are a regular feature.

Pinnacle

We have all tasted the joys of reaching the pinnacle in a physical way, whether winning a school championship or going on a Hemkund Sahib trek. The real taste lies not in overcoming nature or men, but in climbing to the top within.

When you can tell the mind sit and it sits, and when we tell it to breathe, it takes long and deep breaths, know that you are on track and the real battle is going to be won soon.

Grace

Grace is much more than food and cannot be had on a full belly. Only intense longing can shower the grace, only the grace born of utter helplessness stays.

18 WHEAT

An ear of wheat, the golden grain of Punjab, is a joy to hold in one's fingers.

Visiting a farm and spending time in the generous home of the farmer is a rewarding experience. And doing a bit of farming on the side as a hobby establishes an unseen connection with the subtle forces and keeps one humble and down-to-earth.

In the end, when grace has showered on you, and you have felt your arrogance melt, your sorrows wiped out, success kissing your feet, and your heart purified, it's time to give back to nature and live contentedly.

Epilogue

सर्वे भवन्तु सुखिनः । सर्वे सन्तु निरामयाः । सर्वे भद्राणि पश्यन्तु ।

मा कश्चिद् दुःख भाग् भवेत् ॥ ॐ शान्तिः शान्तिः शान्तिः ॥

When faith has blossomed in life, Every step is led by the Divine.

Sri Sri Ravi Shankar

Om Namah Shivaya

जय गुरुदेव